James A. Quick
and His House in Gaylord

Kenneth Lingaur

Lingaur Preservation LLC
Clare, Michigan
2018

James A. Quick and His House in Gaylord

Copyright © 2018 by Kenneth Lingaur

No part of this book may be reproduced in any manner, except with the written permission of Kenneth Lingaur.

Lingaur Preservation LLC
Clare, Michigan
www.lingaurpreservation.com
Printed in the U.S.A.

ISBN-13: 978-1-7322263-1-9
ISBN-10: 1-7322263-1-8

Cover design by Heather Todd

*To my mother,
Eunice Lingaur
we share a love of history.*

Table of Contents

Acknowledgements 1
Introduction 3
James A. Quick 5
The Quick House 19
Dr. Harry Wilson Knapp 22
Dr. George Lucien Cornell 23
Dr. William F. Housen 24
Dr. Charles G. Saunders 25
Architecture 27
General Description of the Quick House 31
Quick House Pre-Rehab Floor Plans 37
Bibliography 39

Acknowledgements

First, I would like to thank Gary Scott, the owner of the James A. Quick House. He took a chance at hiring me, a man with little experience, to write a National Register of Historic Places Nomination and a Federal Historic Tax Credit application for this property. Thank you for your faith in me.

Phil Alexander from the Otsego County Historical Society was a great help at providing historic photographs and providing content suggestions. He went above and beyond what I had hoped for.

Bob Christensen from the Michigan State Historic Preservation Office was instrumental in the final edits of the National Register of Historic Places Nomination for the Quick House. Much of the text for this book came from the nomination.

Finally, I am thankful for my wife, Sherrie, who is a constant source of encouragement and support in everything I do.

Introduction

On August 4, 2016, the house located at 120 North Center Street in Gaylord, Michigan, was officially listed on the National Register of Historic Places. The historic name given to the house is the James A. and Lottie J. (Congdon) Quick House. The house is locally significant for the reasons listed in the Significance Statement of the Nomination:

> The house at 120 North Center Street is significant under national register criterion B for its association with James A. Quick. Mr. Quick was a successful businessman during the late nineteenth and early twentieth century in Gaylord. On his own and in partnership with his brother Charles Quick and another local businessman, Almon Comstock, James A. Quick was involved in a broad variety of businesses in Gaylord and the surrounding area a livery stable, general stores, and banking and he also invested in local real estate, owned and developed local property that included a hotel/boarding house building located near his house. The James A. Quick House is also significant under criterion C as one of Gaylord's most distinguished and intact Queen Anne homes.

As the author of the nomination, I decided to write a book to share this information with others. It takes the text from the National Register of Historic Places Nomination, with some edits, and tells the story of James Quick. Many of the historic photographs and newspaper clippings featured here were not included in the nomination, but are added to tell the story. Some of the historic photographs included may not be of the best quality, but I believe a bad picture is better than no picture. Enjoy learning about James A. Quick and his house in Gaylord.

James A. Quick

James A. Quick was born in Oakland County, Michigan, on October 7, 1857. He lived and worked on his father's farm until he moved to the Gaylord area in 1881, following his older brother Charles A. Quick, who moved to Gaylord in 1879.

Gaylord, which is located in the northern part of Michigan's Lower Peninsula, was rich in timber in the mid-nineteenth century. In the mid-1860s the first explorations of the area were made by timber cruisers looking for marketable timber. In 1869 Charles Brink looked to set up a lumber operation on the southeast corner of Otsego Lake, a few miles south of today's Gaylord, but the location proved to be too remote and the effort was abandoned. Full scale cutting of timber would have to wait until a railroad served the region.

James Alexander Quick
Photograph from
Gaylord Illustrated, 1907
Courtesy of the Otsego
County Historical Society
Collection

The Jackson, Lansing and Saginaw Railroad was the first railroad line built in this area. It was built as far north as Otsego Lake in 1873. In anticipation of the railroad being built farther north, the town of Barnes was platted in 1874 by Orlando M. Barnes of Lansing. He was a leading figure in the railroad's management, serving as the company's secretary and, beginning in 1872, land commissioner. When the railroad was completed to Barnes in 1874, the place was renamed Gaylord in honor of Augustine Smith Gaylord, who then served as the railroad's attorney. Three years later, in 1877, the county seat was moved from Otsego Lake Village to Gaylord.

In 1881, the year James Quick moved to Gaylord, the town was incorporated as a village. It had a population of 400, but was experiencing a boom in growth due to the railroad connection and the line's extension north toward Mackinac, which was just beginning. James Quick purchased an eighty-acre farm just outside of Gaylord. Quick's obituary states that about two years after Charles' 1879 arrival, "in 1881 James A. Quick came to Gaylord to

Quick Brothers Livery, 1880s
Photograph from the Otsego County Historical Society Collection

engage in business with his brother, C. A. Quick, the two having arranged to establish a livery stable here. Immediately following the arrival of James A. Quick the two set to work to procure the timber and erect a suitable barn and arrange for the conduct of the livery business which they succeeded in establishing in the early part of 1883." Their livery barn was located directly across the street from the future Quick residence on North Center Street.

The obituary reports that James and Charles Quick continued their livery barn partnership for about eight years (until about 1891) and then disposed of the business while retaining ownership of the building (though the State Gazetteers list the Quick Brothers Livery through the 1895 edition). They then, the obituary states, relocated to Gould City in Mackinac County in the eastern Upper Peninsula and under the Quick Brothers name operated a "mercantile business" there for about four years, then sold that store and returned to Gaylord.

In 1896 the brothers purchased property in down-

Quick Brothers Store Advertisement
Otsego County Times
January 9, 1903

Quick Brothers Store Building, circa 1920s
Northwest Corner of Main and Center Streets
Photograph Courtesy of Jan White
from the Otsego County Historical Society Collection

Quick Brothers Store, New Toledo
Photograph from the Otsego County Historical Society Collection

town Gaylord and opened a new Quick Brothers Store. The 1897 State Gazetteer is the first to list their Gaylord general store. This store was located at the northwest corner of Main and Center Streets. They also had a general store at New Toledo, later called Quick, a lumber camp located about seven miles to the east and one mile south of Gaylord. When the federal government established a post office in New Toledo in 1899 it was located in the Quick Brothers Store. The establishment of a post office required a change in the place's name since there was already a New Toledo in Michigan, and there could not be two post offices with the same name. The place acquired the name Quick, and James Quick became the first Postmaster, serving until his death.

Another business partnership of James Quick's involved his brother Charles Quick along with another Gaylord businessman, Almon B. C. Comstock. A. B. C Comstock arrived in Gaylord one year before Charles Quick in 1878. Upon his arrival he opened a hardware and tin shop. The current brick building at the northeast corner of Court and Main Streets was constructed by him after the wood frame building he operated out of was destroyed by fire. Comstock was involved in politics, being elected as the supervisor of

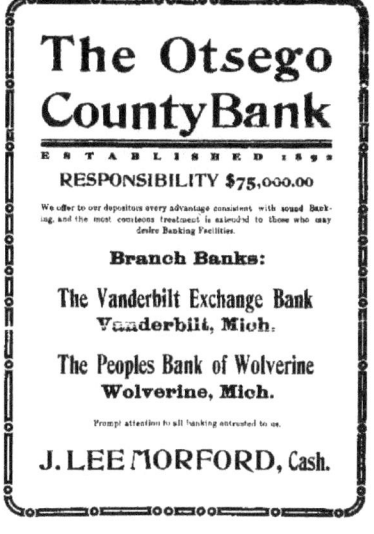

Otsego County Bank Advertisement
Otsego County Times December 7, 1906

Livingston Township, in which most of Gaylord was located, three times, and also served as chairman of the Otsego County Poor Board.

James and Charles Quick and A. B. C. Comstock together established Gaylord's second bank, the Otsego County Bank, in 1892. The older bank in town was the Gaylord Exchange Bank. Another bank, the Gaylord State Savings Bank, followed the next year. Although the Gaylord State Savings Bank would grow to be larger than the Otsego County Bank, the Otsego County Bank was

A. B. C. Comstock Building, circa 1920s
Northeast corner of Main and Court Streets
The Comstock Hardware store was located on the left,
The Otsego County Bank was located on the right.
Photograph from the Otsego County Historical Society Collection

still significant to the community. Advertisements for the bank in the first decade of the twentieth century publicized the bank's responsibilities at $75,000. The Gaylord State Savings Bank on the other hand had deposits of $200,000 as of 1905. By 1907 another Gaylord businessman, J. Lee Morford, also became a partner (and also was then serving as the bank's cashier). The Quicks, Comstock, and Morford also established as branches of the bank the Vanderbilt Exchange Bank at Vanderbilt, eight miles north of Gaylord, in 1905, and the Peoples Bank of Wolverine at Wolverine, ten miles north of Vanderbilt in the southwest corner of Cheboygan County, in 1906. All three banks proved to be successful. The Otsego County Bank, although sound financially, was sold to the Gaylord State Savings Bank in 1919. The Vanderbilt Exchange Bank continued into the 1950s, and the Peoples Bank of Wolverine operated until the early part of the 1910s.

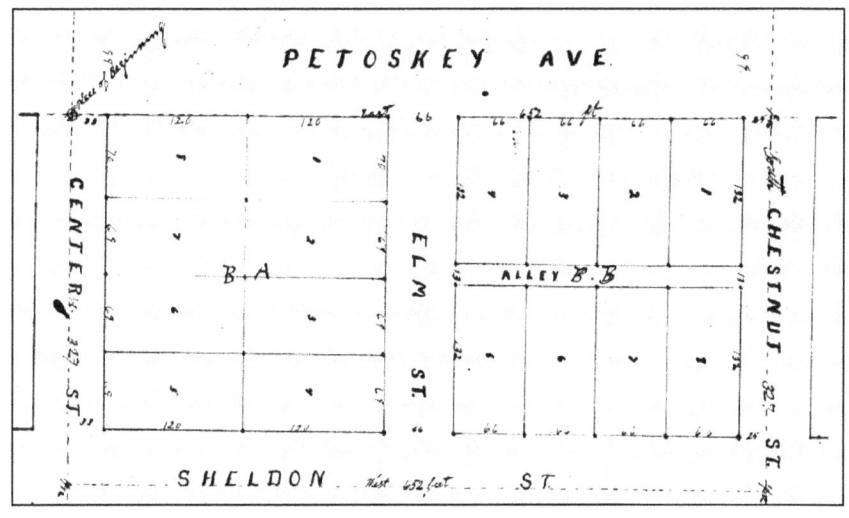

Comstock and Quick's Addition to the Village of Gaylord
Drawing from Comstock and Quick Addition Plat Map

The James Quick, Charles Quick and A. B. C. Comstock partnership was also active in the area of real estate. The most significant of their real estate activities for Gaylord itself was the platting of the Comstock and Quick Addition to the city in 1905. This sixteen-lot subdivision was bounded by Petoskey Avenue, Sheldon Street, Center Street, and the no longer existing Chestnut Street. Real estate, in general, was a major money maker for Quick. Whether solely, in partnership with his brother Charles, or in partnership with Charles and A. B. C. Comstock, James Quick profited through his real estate investments, which included over 1,300 acres of land along with numerous city lots in Gaylord, Vanderbilt, Wolverine, and also property in the "Wah Wah Soo Pleasure Resort" located along the center of the east side of Otsego Lake. It was a resort for the more well-to-do members of the Village of Gaylord.

Another of his investments was in a building located on the lot directly south of his house on North Center Street. When Quick acquired the three-story building is unclear, but several newspaper notices during 1906 and 1907 make references to it. The building is not shown on the 1898 Sanborn Map, but does appear along with Quick's House on the 1907 map. The May 4, 1906, *Otsego County Times* reported that "Workmen are just now putting the finishing touches" on the building, which Quick "has been remodeling for the past six weeks." The building was to become Mrs. Frank Mack's boarding house. The following month (June 22) the *Times* noted that Mrs. Mack's "hotel and boarding house" would be called the Delmont. Quick's building suffered a fire sometime

Delmont Hotel, in background of photograph, circa 1920
Photograph from the Otsego County Historical Society Collection

around May 1907 by which it was "partially destroyed," but was being renovated again into a rooming and boarding house as of early June (*Times,* June 7, 1907). In September 1907 Quick leased the Delmont for three years to Frank Wransky of Traverse City, "for many years connected with the Park Place hotel" there (*Times*, September 2, 1907). The Delmont Hotel continued to operate until the 1920s and was known as "the business man's hotel." The building no longer stands.

In 1902 James Quick's ill health caused him to withdraw from active business. He sold his interest in the Quick Brothers Store in 1903 to his brother Charles, who continued it until 1912, when he sold out to Leon and Harry Parmater. Quick's obituary stated that "Since 1902 Mr. Quick has not been actively engaged in any business except to interest himself in the buggy and cutter business in a small way from time to time more as a matter of occupying his attention than as a matter of real business." Quick bought out the vehicle and cutter stock from another local firm in 1906 and, according to a brief newspaper notice from July, is "making a considerable bustle for the business" (*Times*, July 20, 1906). After adding to his stock of vehicles in 1907 he moved his business from the Cook Brothers building on Main Street to the old Quick Brothers livery barn across the street from his residence on Center Street.

Despite James Quick's illness in 1902 and the comment in his

James A. Quick
Advertisement from
Otsego County Times
May 31, 1907

obituary about him not being actively engaged in business thereafter, he did not disengage himself from the affairs of the Gaylord community. In 1903 he was elected to a three-year term on the village council, and was re-elected to a two-year term in 1906. This was not his first experience with public office. At some prior unknown time he held the position of Livingston Township Treasurer.

As a Village Trustee, Quick served on both the Water & Light Committee and the License Committee all of his five years on the Council. He also served on the Fire Department, Rules, and Street Committees during differing years of his service. His time on the Village Council was noted for its upgrading of the village's infrastructure. Those improvements included the construction of a two-inch galvanized gas pipe with "T" connections to each lot within the village starting in 1903. In 1905, the Council passed a resolution that all new sidewalks be constructed of cement. That same year the sidewalk in front of the Quick residence was constructed. Although James Quick was not on the Street Committee that worked on the sidewalk resolution, he was on the committee the following year, 1906, when the Council voted to discontinue the Village of Gaylord's role in constructing sidewalks. Instead of directly building sidewalks, the village encouraged the construction of more sidewalks by authorizing a tax rebate of two and one half cents per square foot to any citizen who undertook the replacement or new construction of a cement sidewalk.

A major upgrade of the village's water system was the main accomplishment of the Village Council while James

James A. Quick
Otsego County Times
September 20, 1907

Quick was a trustee. The replacement of the water storage tank took place in 1906, and new water pumps were installed and connected in January 1907. The original water storage tank was located on the lot immediately to the east of James Quick's residence. After the old water tank was removed the village authorized the sale of the lot where it was located, and James Quick obtained the lot by submitting his sealed bid.

As part of the License Committee, James Quick assisted in writing the first village ordinance restricting the sale of alcohol within the village limits. The ordinance raised the fee necessary to obtain a liquor license in the Village to $500. The State of Michigan already required a fee of $500 for a liquor license, and this additional fee would bring the total to $1,000. Permission from the state legislature was required for this provision of the ordinance, which was easily obtained. In addition, the ordinance limited the number of liquor licenses issued to businesses within the Village of Gaylord to six.

In addition to his business and political interests James Quick also devoted some of his attention to farming. Although he was not actively involved with the day-to-day activities of the farm he purchased in 1882, he was nonetheless involved in its overall operation. By the time of his death the eighty-acre farm had been expanded to one hundred and sixty acres. James' interest

> James Quick has a private toboggan slide upon which he sometimes enjoys himself. Monday he was on his barn and shoveled the snow from the "flat roof" part. He then went down a short ladder to the "leanto" part. This is where the toboggan slide begins. It ends in about a foot of slush behind the barn.
>
> *Otsego County Times*
> *February 16, 1906*

in farming also led him to serve as president of the Otsego County Agricultural Society in 1906 and 1907. The purpose of the society was to plan for and hold the annual county fair. From the *Otsego County Times* write-up of the 1906 fair, it would seem the fair was ordinary when compared to previous years. However, the paper's 1907 summary of the fair was much longer and much more enthusiastic. The paper exclaimed that it was "Bigger and Better than Ever." Quick's success with the county fair resulted in him being named to head the committee which prepared the Otsego County exhibit for the Michigan State Fair. This was a position he held in 1907 and 1908.

During his life James A. Quick was considered one of the prominent citizens of Gaylord. The *Otsego County Times* printed a special edition in September 1905 for the purpose of attracting new manufacturing industries and settlers to purchase unimproved farm lands in the area. A photograph of James along with a short bio and a photograph of his residence were featured in this edition of the paper. Two years later a small picture pamphlet, *Gaylord Illustrated*, which featured important people and buildings in Gaylord, also featured Quick and his residence.

James Quick married Lottie J. Congdon on Thanksgiving Day 1895. They had no children except for a daughter, Juliette Leona, who they adopted when she was very young. He was a member of the Gaylord Lodge of the Free & Accepted Masons, Order of the Eastern Stars, Masonic Benefit Association, Maccabees and Knights of Pythias, and the Gaylord Congregational Church. His illness in 1902 left him in a weakened state that he never fully recovered from. As a result later in life, after being ill for two weeks, he passed away from typhoid fever on September 8, 1909. He died at the age of fifty-two. He was survived by two brothers, Charles and Adrian, both of Gaylord and a sister Mrs. Mary A. Brosiur of Genesee County. He was preceded in death by a brother, Abram Quick who was killed by a cyclone in 1896. James Quick's body was taken to his former home in Oakland County for burial at the Ortonville Cemetery. His wife Lottie would later remarry to Charles Albert Horton, and they lived in Flint, Michigan (the second marriage for both of them). Lottie lived until 1937, when she died at the age of 67. She is buried in the Ortonville Cemetery next to her first husband James Quick.

The Quick House

James A. Quick House at 120 North Center Street
Photograph from Gaylord Illustrated, 1907
Courtesy of the Otsego County Historical Society Collection

A review of the local tax records suggests that James A. Quick's house at 120 North Center Street was built in 1900. The lot he built the house on was purchased jointly by him and his brother Charles in January 1890. It was not until January 1903 that James bought out Charles' interest in the property. This was the same time that James Quick sold his interest in the Quick Brothers business to his brother Charles.

James Quick lived in his house from the time of its construction until his early death at the age of fifty-two in 1909. His wife Lottie Quick took over his business activities after his death, besides the running of her Gaylord millinery store which she opened in 1906. By August 1912 she had sold her millinery business and opened a new millinery store in the Detroit area. She continued to manage the business affairs of her former husband into the 1920s. After her move to Detroit the house sat vacant for about one year. In October 1913, Dr. Harry Knapp (see page 22) purchased the house with the intent of using it for his residence and medical office. In November 1913, Dr. Knapp constructed a separate entrance for his patients on the house's south side. Dr. Knapp sold the house in March 1919 to Dr. William Housen, a local dentist (see page 24), and owned it for two years. Another dentist, Dr. Charles Saunders (see page 25), purchased the house in June 1921. Dr. Saunders lived there for forty-nine years until his death in 1970. Charles Saunders practiced dentistry in the house at the start of his ownership, but by 1936 he relocated his dental practice to an office above the Audrain Hardware Store in Gaylord. The 1968-1969 Gaylord City Directory

PRICES ON MILLINERY GOODS GREATLY REDUCED!

On Saturday, March 17, we will place on sale a large stock of

LADIES' STREET HATS, CHILDREN'S CAPS and CHILDREN'S SCHOOL HATS.

We must close out these to make room for the Spring Stock. Don't fail to look in during this sale (it lasts only ten days) and see if you will not be able to find a genuine bargain.

Mrs. Lottie Quick,

OPPOSITE COURT HOUSE,   GAYLORD, MICH.

Mrs. Lottie Quick Millinery Advertisement Otsego County Times March 16, 1906

lists him as practicing dentistry out of the house once again. It was Dr. Saunders who constructed the addition on the southeast corner of the house. The 1948 Sanborn map does not show the addition, and no newspaper articles have been located to indicate when the addition was constructed. However, tax records suggest the addition was constructed in 1950. After the death of Dr. Saunders his second wife Helen (known more commonly by her middle name Elizabeth) continued to live in the house until her death in 1999. After her death the house was vacant for a number of years. Tamara Reeme purchased it in October 1999, and then sold it to JGLA Investments in August 2010. Applegate Building, owned by Gary Scott, purchased the house in August 2013 and later conducted a substantial rehabilitation.

> On Tuesday August 24, 1909 Mr. Claude Shannon Sr. secretly left Gaylord on the midnight train. Unknown to anyone he was on his way to Lansing to marry Miss Mabel Wolf. The two were married the following evening at the Wolf residence. Most people, who knew the couple, had knowledge that they would wed before September 1st, but only a very few knew the exact date. Mr. Shannon was, at the time of their wedding, the owner of a local furniture store, while his bride was a teacher at the Gaylord High School. After their return to Gaylord the couple intended to live in the home of James and Lottie Quick. One month later James Quick would pass away.
> Information from "Shannon – Wolf Nuptials"
> *Otsego County Times*, August 27, 1909

Dr. Harry Wilson Knapp

Harry Knapp was born on August 9, 1872, but it is unknown where he originated from. He married Mary Cornell, who was born February 19, 1871. Harry Knapp graduated from the Detroit College of Medicine in 1903. He worked his way through medical school by serving as a purser aboard the ships "City of Holland" and "Pilgrim." Both ships were owned by the Thompson Freight and Passenger Steamboat Line and had a regular route between Detroit and Rogers City. After graduating from medical school, he located to Johannesburg where he practiced as a physician and surgeon. He practiced medicine there until he relocated to Gaylord

Dr. Harry Knapp, 1903
Photograph from the Otsego County Herald Times March 14, 1929

Dr. H. W. Knapp
Advertisement
Otsego County Herald and Times

in 1913, when he purchased this house from Lottie Quick.

Harry Knapp was called to serve in the Army Medical Corps., in the summer of 1918. He was given the rank of Captain and first served at Camp Perry in Ohio. In October 1918 he was transferred to Camp Zachery Taylor in Louisville, Kentucky. He was discharged from the army in January 1919 and relocated to Flint instead of moving back to Gaylord. He practiced medicine in Flint until his sudden death by heart attack at the age of fifty-nine in 1931.

Dr. George Lucien Cornell

George Cornell was the brother of Harry Knapp's wife, Mary. When Harry was called to the army in 1918 George and his wife Alice moved into this house. Both George and Alice were born in Prince Edward, Ontario. George was born in 1864 and Alice was born in 1849. Like Harry Knapp, George was also a doctor, but he specialized in "obstetrics and diseases of women and children." George and Alice lived in the house until April 1919 when Harry Knapp sold the house to William Housen. They continued to live in Gaylord for a number of years. Alice would pass away in 1925 while

DR. G. L. CORNELL
Physician and Surgeon
Successor to Dr. Knapp
Office and Residence in the
DR. KNAPP HOME

Dr. G. L. Cornell
Advertisement
Otsego County Advance

living in Gaylord. George would later move away from Gaylord and remarry. He passed away in 1933.

Dr. William F. Housen

William F. Housen was born in 1885 in Windsor, Ontario. He attended the Detroit Dental College and graduated in 1908. While going through dental school he worked in the composition room of the Detroit News. He came to Gaylord in August 1908 and set up his practice on the second floor of the Comstock building in downtown Gaylord. In October of the same year he moved his office to the second floor of the Brodie & Qua building.

Housen had a love for the game of basketball. He was the boy's high school coach for a number of years and also refereed many games.

He was elected as a Village Trustee in 1917, but was not able to complete his term. In 1918, he was ordered to Camp Sherman, Ohio to serve as a dentist for the U. S. Army's 95th Division. He served with the rank of Lieutenant. Housen was discharged in December 1918 and returned to Gaylord. Three months later he purchased this house from Harry Knapp. He lived here until 1921 when he sold the house to Dr. Charles Saunders. Dr. Housen then moved to Detroit where he practiced dentistry until his death in 1935 at the age of fifty.

Dr. Charles G. Saunders

Charles G. Saunders was born on May 5, 1887 in Stanton, Michigan. He attended the Detroit College of Medicine and began his dental practice in Wolverine, Michigan in 1907. He came to Gaylord in 1921 when he purchased this house from Dr. William Housen. The July 7, 1907 issue of the *Otsego County Herald & Times* reported the following about Dr. Saunders opening a dental practice in Gaylord:

Mr. Saunders comes here recommended as one of the very best dentists in all the north part of the state in fact in all the state. It is said that his customers come from as far south as Bay City and north to Mackinaw, which speaks well for his work.

Charles first wife was named Elsie. She originated from Sanilac County and was born April 14, 1879. Elsie passed away in 1943, and Charles remarried in 1952 to Helen Elizabeth Wilkinson. Elizabeth was born in Gaylord on May 27, 1907.

In addition to owning this house, Charles Saunders also owned a 1,300 acre ranch on the Black River. The ranch included a "lodge, barns, two saddle horses, 80 cattle and a place to get away from civilization."

Dr. Saunders was a member of the Gaylord Masonic Lodge, Bay City Consistory, Elf Khurafeh Temple of Saginaw, Life Member of the American Dental Association, and a Life Member of the Michigan State Dental Association. He passed away on October 13, 1970.

Quick House, circa mid-1950s
Elizabeth and Dr. Charles Saunders, owners
Photograph from the Otsego County Historical Society Collection

Architecture

Quick House, early 1920s
Dr. Charles and Elsie Saunders, owners
Photograph from the Otsego County Historical Society Collection

The James A. Quick House is a well-preserved Queen Anne wood frame house. The house was illustrated in the *Otsego County Times* September 1905 Gaylord special edition and the 1907 *Gaylord Illustrated* publication – thus evidently considered one of the town's showpiece homes when it was new. It is also one of the few "high style" homes from the turn of the twentieth century or prior to still exist in Gaylord.

The Queen Anne style was popular in the United States from approximately 1880 to 1910. The style was very loosely modeled after the later nineteenth-century English domestic architecture of architect Richard Norman Shaw and others. The 1874 Watts-Sherman House in Newport, Rhode Island, is generally considered the first Queen Anne house in America. Queen Anne houses in America typically displayed irregular, rambling footprints with tall hip and gable roofs and exterior finishes that emphasized variety in cladding materials and an abundance of ornamentation. While the largest and finest American examples often exhibited walls faced in brick and stone along with gables and other areas clad in stucco, slate, and ornamental wood shingling, the style was soon translated via local designers and pattern books into smaller scale house forms that, entirely constructed and finished in wood, used traditional American clapboarding along with patterned shingling accents in upper façade areas and gables and turned spindlework used for porches and often in gables.

The Queen Anne style is known for the variation in surface textures, and also the different ways in which flat surfaces were broken up. The Quick House is mostly clad with beaded horizontal clapboard siding, but it is also ornamented with diamond, fishscale and hexagonal-butt shingling. The patterned shingling forms decorative accents in the north and south sides, within the second-story front porch gable, and within the gable over the front porch's corner entry. The otherwise roughly rectangular house form is broken up through gabled projections on both sides, a bay window, extensive wraparound porch, and second-story gabled front porch.

The interior of the James Quick House has remained largely unchanged since the 1950s, and also retains much of its original features. The dominant wood finish found in the first floor of the house is tiger maple. Tiger maple, also known as curly maple, gets its name from what appears to be curls or stripes in the grain pattern along the length of the board. Because of the process of quarter sawing wood to achieve the best appearance of curls, tiger maple is more expensive than ordinary wood.

The windows in the house's entryway and dining room display unusually large size sashes. Most one-over-one windows have equally sized upper and lower sashes. The sashes in these two rooms of the Quick House have lower sashes that are approximately double the size of the upper sashes.

Quick House Attic showing structural bracing, 2015
Photograph from the Author's Collection

The structural bracing found in the attic is another distinctive feature of this house. This zig-zag bracing with metal tie rods gives strength to the entire house. The bracing supports the front facing gable to the point that the two columns on the balcony do not bear any weight. At the same time the columns on the wraparound porch bear only a minimal amount of weight.

The house's designer is unknown. Another house only a few blocks away at 210 E. Main Street, built in 1900 for Dr. Abraham Simmons, is a mirror image of the Quick House, though with siding and all other finishes now clad in vinyl material that obscures or replaced all of the historic exterior finishes. Although no primary source can be found as to who was the builder of the Quick House, one source lists him as William Powers. Little is known of William Powers, but he is found in the 1900 census as living in nearby Livingston Township, with his occupation listed as contractor/builder.

North Center Street historically was one of the streets in Gaylord where a number of leading and prosperous citizens of the village lived. Heading north on North Center Street from Main at the east edge of the downtown, the James Quick House is the first of the larger homes encountered along the street. Other large Queen Anne houses on North Center Street include the E. B. Bolton House at 135 North Center, the Sanford Buck House at 206 North Center, the J. M. Brodie House at 207 North Center, and the Frank Kramer House at 221 North Center. The Bolton House now serves as a funeral home, with a modern much expanded ground story and other substantial alterations, the Buck House was being extensively renovated in 2016, and the Brodie House also has synthetic siding that obscures most historic exterior finishes. Of the other large houses along the street, only the Frank Kramer House, listed on the National Register of Historic Places in 2002, retains a high degree of integrity. The Kramer House is Gaylord's most highly decorative Queen Anne home.

General Description of the Quick House

The house is located in a mixed residential and commercial area on the first block of North Center Street north of Main Street. The east-west-running Main Street comprises the heart of Gaylord's downtown commercial area. Center Street intersects Main at the east end of the downtown area. At the time of the house's construction the commercial area of Gaylord was located to the south and southwest along Main Street, and the buildings to the north, west and east were primarily residential. Since then the commercial area of Gaylord has grown to the north

Entryway of Quick House prior to rehabilitation, 2015
Photograph from the Author's Collection

Dining Room of Quick House prior to rehabilitation, 2015
Photograph from the Author's Collection

along Center Street. At present the part of North Center in which the house is located contains a mixture of modern commercial development and older homes, some of them converted to commercial use and substantially altered. The Quick House property backs up to residential development to its east.

The Quick House is a two-story Queen Anne house that stands on a stone foundation and is topped by a hip roof with lower cross gables. The foundation is primarily of uncoursed fieldstone, while the visible stones on the foundation's north and south exterior elevations are dressed. The building is clad in beaded wood clapboard siding and a variety of types of wood shingling. The roof is covered with faux diamond slate asphalt shingles

Addition to Quick House prior to rehabilitation, 2015
Photograph from the Author's Collection

applied over cedar shingles. The front of the house faces west and features a hip-roof porch across the entire west façade on the first story that wraps around to the north elevation east as far as the house's gabled north projection.

The house's interior has retained much of its original appearance. The woodwork, which is primarily tiger maple, has never been painted. The wood floors in the entryway, dining room, and front parlor are finished in concentric squares with alternating maple and oak wood planks. The remainder of the house also retains its wood flooring except for the kitchen and bathrooms. The second story wood trim is made of pine. The house has also kept its original cast iron floor and wall registers. The walls are finished in plaster on wood lathe and were covered with

Exterior of Quick House prior to rehabilitation, 2015
Photograph from the Author's Collection

wallpaper. Much of that wallpaper and some light fixtures dated from the mid-twentieth century. The walls in the addition are covered with paneled wood and the ceiling is coffered. Prior to the rehabilitation the interior close to the addition and the east end of the house showed evidence of alterations. Much of this evidence existed in the form of mismatched woodwork and light fixtures that were not centered in rooms. A second stairway at the east end of the house along with a door separating the east end of the second floor is evidence that the house was constructed with the idea of having a servant living there. An electronic stair lift was added to the east end stairway at an unknown date.

The Quick House has seen considerable changes to its appearance since its original construction, though some of these changes have now been reversed. The changes were mostly seen in the siding and the porches, which occurred in the mid-twentieth century. The house was originally clad with its existing wood clapboard and shingle siding, but this was covered by asbestos siding in the mid-twentieth century. The first story was covered with a faux brick siding and the second with a faux shake shingle siding. The wraparound porch originally extended across the entire façade of the building and was supported by Tuscan columns, with the columns occurring singly and in pairs. Some of the columns were removed and the remainder boxed in and covered with the faux brick siding in the mid-twentieth century. All the asbestos siding was removed in October 2015. The fronts of the wraparound porch and balcony were originally enclosed with simple low spindle balustrades. The porch at the east end of the north elevation also contained spindlework spandrels and turned columns. The stairways to the wraparound and northeast corner porches featured wooden newel posts with spindlework balusters. The gables including the gable over the front corner porch entry of the wraparound porch were ornamented with decorative bargeboard, and finials were found at the apexes of each gable. The same finials were found at the east and west ends of the hipped roof's apex. All these decorative pieces were removed when the asbestos siding was added in the mid-twentieth century. A raised line of shingles encircled the lower part of the roof. The roof was originally covered with cedar shingles. All the current doors and windows are original features of the house with the exception of the large window on the south projection's south elevation, which was a mid-twentieth-century addition.

A concrete sidewalk extends along the north elevation of the house from the northeast corner porch to the sidewalk along Center Street. The sidewalk along Center Street was not constructed until 1905. A portion of the sidewalk originally extended beyond the Center Street sidewalk and contained a small monument with the lettering "J A QUICK." An additional sidewalk ran from the Center Street sidewalk to the entrance of the addition on the south elevation of the house.

At the northeast corner of the property stands a one-story hip-roof garage. The garage's front faces north, fronting on Huron Street. The garage was constructed sometime between 1907 and 1916. According to the Sanborn maps the west two-thirds of the garage was originally two-story and the east one-third one-story. It is uncertain as to when the garage was changed from two to one-story.

The Sanborn Maps also indicate the existence of either a gasoline pump or tank on Huron Street just to the west of the garage. This object was placed on the property between 1916 and 1927. It also appears on the 1948 map, but it is unknown when it was removed.

The Delmont Hotel was also located on the southwest corner of the property from about the turn of the twentieth century to the mid-1920s. This was a three-story building with a two-story rear addition.

James A. Quick House
Pre-rehab First Floor Plan

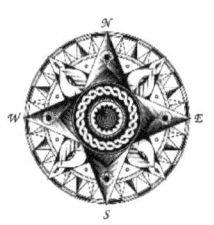

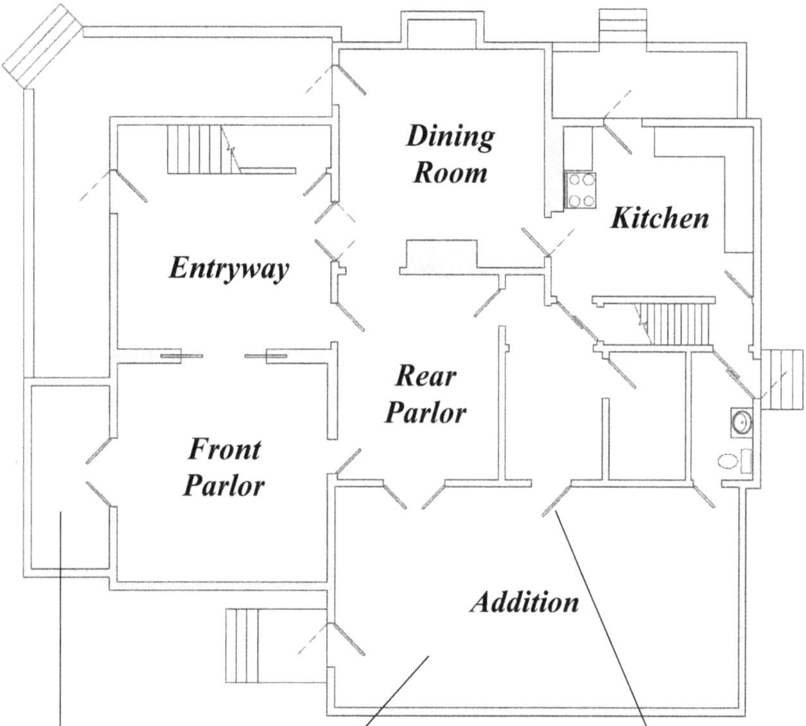

Entryway

Dining Room

Kitchen

Front Parlor

Rear Parlor

Addition

Sun Room and Addition added in the mid-1900s

Possible location where Dr. Knapp constructed door on south side of house in 1913

Floor Plan Drawings
Courtesy of Sidock Group Architects
Gaylord, Michigan

James A. Quick House
Pre-rehab Second Floor Plan

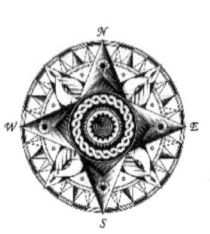

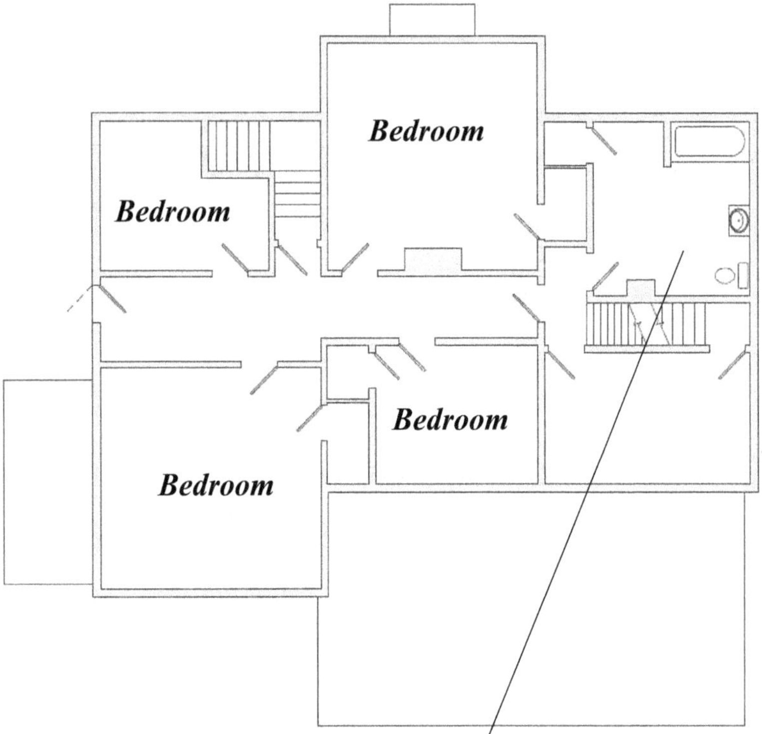

Bedroom

Bedroom

Bedroom

Bedroom

Possible room for servants quarters before being converted to a bathroom in the mid-1900s

Floor Plan Drawings
Courtesy of Sidock Group Architects
Gaylord, Michigan

Bibliography

"348 Ballots Were Cast At Monday's Election." *Otsego County Herald and Times* [Gaylord, MI] Vol. 43 No. 5 ed.: 1. Print.

"1903 to 1907 Meeting Minutes." *Records of the Village Council Proceedings*, Village of Gaylord. Vols 5 and 6. Gaylord, MI: Print.

"A Big Success In Every Way." *Otsego County Times* [Gaylord, MI] 12 Oct. 1906, Vol. 2 No. 10 ed.: 1. Print.

"Additional Locals." *Otsego County Herald* [Gaylord, MI] 16 Jan. 1903, Vol. 28 No. 40 ed.: 8. Print.

"Among Our Friends and Neighbors." *Otsego County Advance* [Gaylord, MI] 25 Oct. 1918, Vol. 8 No. 5. Print.

"Big Water Tank Nearly Completed," *Otsego County Times* [Gaylord, MI] 07 Sept. 1906, Vol. 2 No. 5 ed.: 1. Print.

"C. G. Saunders Now Ready For Business." *Otsego County Herald & Times* [Gaylord, MI] 7 July 1921, Vol. 51 No. 15 ed.: 1. Print.

"City of Holland." *The Evening News* [Detroit, MI] 30 Jan. 1901, Pg. 10. Print.

"Correspondence." *Otsego County Times* [Gaylord, MI] 16 Feb. 1906, Vol. 1 No. 28 ed.: 8. Print.

"Dr. Saunders dies in Gaylord." *Gaylord Herald & Times* [Gaylord, MI] 14 Oct. 1970, Vol. 98 No. 34 ed.: 10. Print.

"Dr. William F. Housen." *Detroit Free Press* [Detroit, MI] 10 Feb. 1935, Yr 104 No 282 ed.: 4. Print.

"Fair Officers Meeting." *Otsego County Times* [Gaylord, MI] 02 Feb. 1906, Vol. 1 No. 26 ed.: 1. Print.

Gaylord Illustrated, Herald Printing House, [Gaylord, MI] 1907.

Gilardy, Patricia, and Beth Warner. "Quick, An Early Lumbering Village." *A Step Back in Time* Vol. 1 (1996): 19-20. Print.

Granland, Bill. "The Vanished Town of New Toledo." *Gaylord Herald Times* 9 Feb. 2002: B-10. Print.

"Helen Elizabeth Saunders." *Gaylord Herald & Times* [Gaylord, MI] 2 June 1999, Vol. 124 No. 12 ed.: B-7 Print.

"It Eclipses Them All." *Otsego County Times* [Gaylord, MI] 20 Sept. 1907, Vol. 3 No 7 ed.: 1+. Print.

"Items In Brief." *Otsego County Herald and Times* [Gaylord, MI] 20 Sept. 1918, Vol. 46 No. 29. Print.

"Items In Brief." *Otsego County Herald and Times* [Gaylord, MI] 25 Oct. 1918, Vol. 46 No. 33. Print.

"Items In Brief." *Otsego County Herald and Times* [Gaylord, MI] 27 Dec. 1918, Vol. 46 No. 42. Print.

"James A. Quick is Dead" *Otsego County Times* [Gaylord, MI] 10 Sept. 1909, Vol. 5, No. 6 ed.: 1. Print.

Jensen Dorothy. "Nothing Better Than Gaylord." *A Step Back in Time 3* (2001): 105. Print.

"Less Saloons In Gaylord." *Otsego County Times* [Gaylord, MI] 26 Apr. 1907, Vol. 2 No. 38 ed.: 1. Print.

Lingaur Kenneth, National Register of Historic Places Nomination: James A. and Lottie J. Congdon) Quick House, Nov. 20, 2015.

"Local Items." *Otsego County Herald & Times* [Gaylord, MI] 26 Jan. 1912, Vol. 36 No. 24 ed.: 9. Print.

"Local Items." *Otsego County Herald & Times* [Gaylord, MI] 30 Aug. 1912, Vol. 38 No. 23 ed.: 5. Print.

"Mrs. G. A. Cornell Died Sunday After Many Years Illness." *Otsego County Herald Times* [Gaylord, MI] 24 Sept. 1925, Vol. 50 No. 27: 1. Print.

"New Engine Running." *Otsego County Times* [Gaylord, MI] 15 Nov. 1907, Vol. 3 No. 15 ed.: 10. Print.

"New Enterprise." *Otsego County Times* [Gaylord, MI] 20 July 1906, Vol. 1 No. 50 ed.: 1. Print

"New Physicians." *The Evening News* [Detroit, MI] 1 May 1903, pg. 7, Print.

"New Hotel Proposition." *Otsego County Times* [Gaylord, MI] 20 Sept. 1907, Vol. 3 No. 7 ed.: 5. Print.

"New Pumps Are Connected." *Otsego County Times* [Gaylord, MI] 25 Jan. 1907, Vol. 2 No. 25 ed.: 1. Print.

"Of Local Interest To Our Readers." *Otsego County Times* [Gaylord, MI] 03 July 1908, Vol. 3 No. 48 ed.: 8. Print.

Robinson's 1968-1969 Gaylord City Directory. Association of North American Directory Publishers: New York, 1968. Print.

"Obituary, Mrs. C. G. Saunders." *Otsego County Herald Times* [Gaylord, MI] 13 May 1943, Vol. 68 No. 9 ed.: 2. Print.

The Otsego County Bank. *Otsego County Herald* 15 Sept. 1905: 2. Print.

"Otsego County Banks Consolidated This Week." *Otsego County Advance* [Gaylord, MI] 21 Aug. 1919, Vol. 8 No. 32 ed.: 1. Print.

Otsego County Register of Deeds. Deed Records. N.d. Land Records data. Otsego County Building, Gaylord, MI.

Otsego County Treasures Office. Tax Records. N.d. Tax data. Otsego County Building, Gaylord, MI.

"Salt and Pepper." *Otsego County Herald Times* [Gaylord, MI] 12 Aug. 1937, Vol. 63 No. 21 ed.: Print.

Sanborn Fire Insurance Map. *Environmental Data Resources*: Sanborn Map Company, Pelham, NY, Gaylord MI. 1898. Sheets 5 & 6. Print.

Sanborn Fire Insurance Map. *Environmental Data Resources*: Sanborn Map Company, Pelham, NY, Gaylord MI. 1907. Sheets 5 & 7. Print.

Sanborn Fire Insurance Map. *Environmental Data Resources*: Sanborn Map Company, Pelham, NY, Gaylord MI. 1916. Sheets 2 & 7. Print

Sanborn Fire Insurance Map. *Environmental Data Resources*: Sanborn Map Company, Pelham, NY, Gaylord MI. 1927. Sheets 2 & 8 Print.

Sanborn Fire Insurance Map. *Environmental Data Resources*: Sanborn Map Company, Pelham, NY, Gaylord MI. 1927/1948. Sheet 2. Print.

"Shannon – Wolf Nuptials." *Otsego County Times* [Gaylord, MI] 27 Aug. 1909, Vol. 5 No. 4 ed.: 1. Print.

"Short Local Items." *Otsego County Times* [Gaylord, MI] 4 May 1906, Vol. 1 No. 39 ed.: 4. Print.

"Short Local Items." *Otsego County Times* [Gaylord, MI] 29 June 1906, Vol. 1 No. 47 ed.: 3. Print.

"Short Local Items." *Otsego County Times* [Gaylord, MI] 7 June 1907, Vol. 2 No. 44 ed.: 2. Print.

"The State Fair." *Otsego County Times* [Gaylord, MI] 15 Mar. 1907, Vol. 2 No. 32 ed.: 2. Print.

"To Camp Perry." *Otsego County Herald and Times* [Gaylord, MI] 30 Aug. 1918, Vol. 46 No. 26. Print.

State of Michigan Archives. Otsego County Tax Records. N.d. Tax data. State of Michigan Archives, Lansing, MI.

"Well Known Man Died Last Thurs." *Otsego County Herald Times* [Gaylord, MI] 15 Oct. 1931, Vol. 57 No. 31. Print.

About the Author

Kenneth Lingaur is a native of Northern Michigan. He spent his early years in Lake Leelanau, Michigan, and has lived in Clare, Michigan since 2003. He earned his Master's Degree in Historic Preservation from Eastern Michigan University in 2014, and the following year founded Lingaur Preservation LLC.

Lingaur Preservation LLC is a historic preservation consulting firm specializing in the research and documentation of historic places.

Ken got his first taste of Gaylord's history while writing the National Register of Historic Places Nomination for the James A. and Lottie J. (Congdon) Quick House. The house was listed on the National Register in 2016.

Ken has been married since 1995, and along with his wife, Sherrie, have four boys.

For more information on Lingaur Preservation LLC visit his website at www.lingaurpreservation.com.

Other Books by Kenneth Lingaur

Clare, Michigan may seem like your ordinary Midwest town, but some of the people that lived here were far from usual. In these pages you will read about a man who was ship wrecked in the middle of the Atlantic Ocean, a couple who missed their trip to America on the Titanic, a man who came to Clare with nothing and became her most famous citizen, and what story about Clare would be complete without gangsters.

Where They Lived chronicles the lives of the people who lived in fifty-one historic Clare homes. After reading this book you will see these houses in a new light, and hopefully appreciate the history behind them.

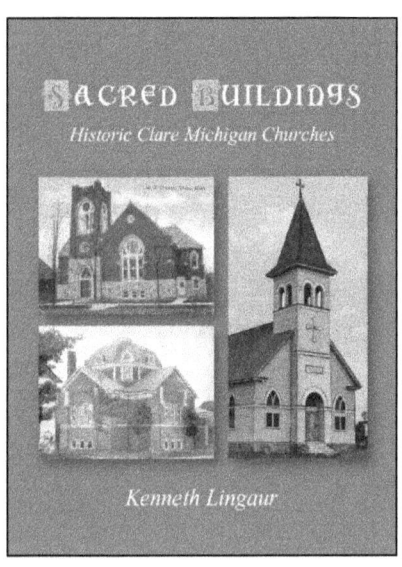

From simple wood frame buildings to a church listed on the National Register of Historic Places, the church buildings in Clare, Michigan are varied.

Spanning from the founding of Clare to the present *Sacred Buildings: Historic Clare Michigan Churches* tells the story of seventeen different church buildings from thirteen congregations.

This is the story of the places that the people of Clare built to share their common faith and worship their God.

Sacred Buildings: Historic Clare Michigan Churches is full of photographs and descriptions which take you inside many of these buildings.

These books are available at Amazon.com and local Clare, Michigan retailers

www.ingramcontent.com/pod-product-compliance
Lightning Source LLC
Chambersburg PA
CBHW061301040426
42444CB00010B/2470